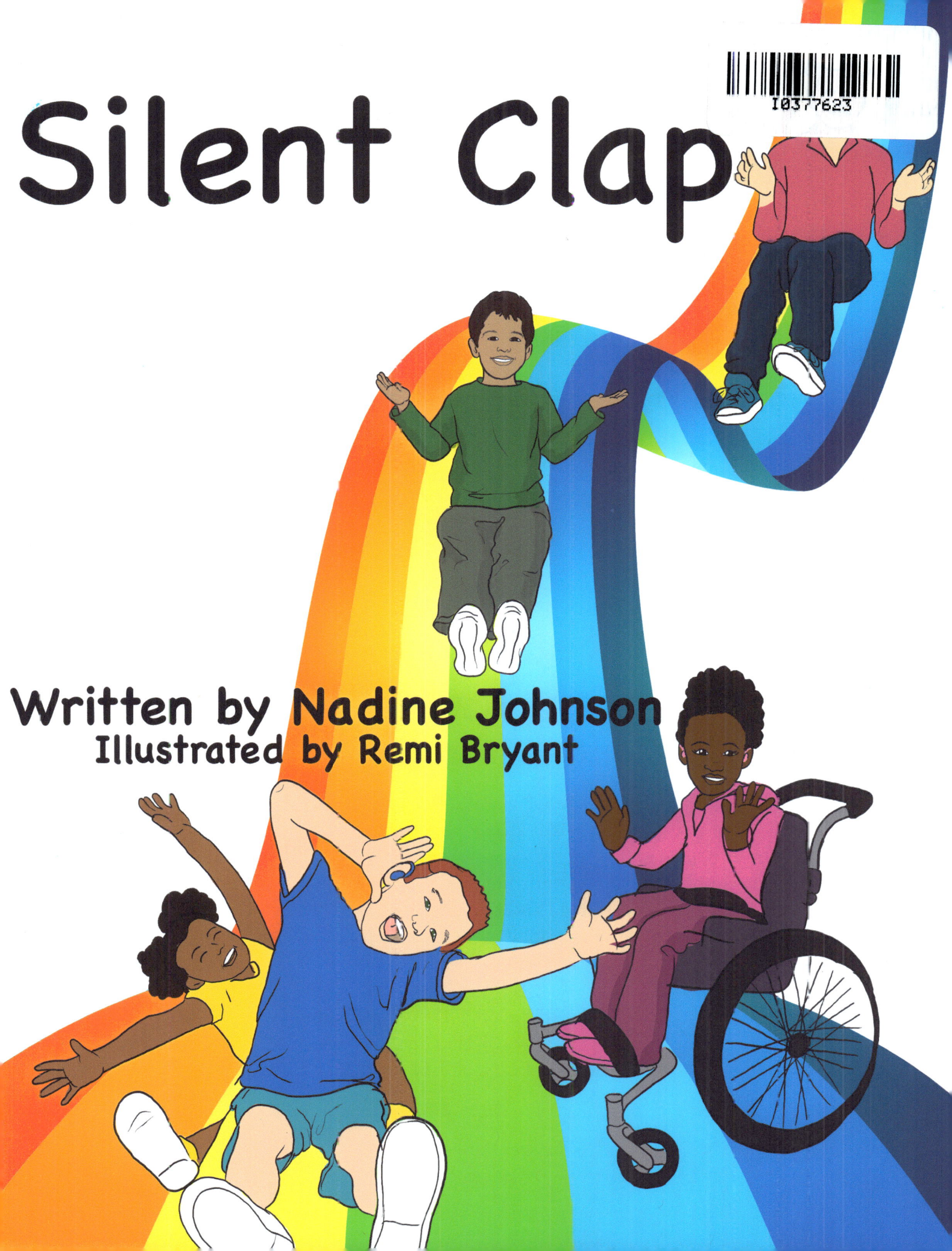

Silent Clap. All rights reserved.
Copyright 2021 © Nadine Johnson

No part of this book may be reproduced in any form or by any electronic or mechanical means, including information storage and retrieval systems, without the permission in writing from the author. However, reviewers may quote brief passages in a review. Contact author at nadinegio18@gmail.com.

ISBN: 978-1-954529-17-5 First Edition
ISBN: 9798486378416 Second Edition
eBook ISBN: 9781954529281

Published by PlayPen Publishing
PlayPenPublishing.com
United States

Acknowledgments

To my son, Geovaughnie Wilson, thank you for helping me conceptualize my books.

To Natalie Dawkins (sissy), thank you for proofreading the contents within this book.

To Jhevaugh Johnson and Marva Dixon, thank you for always motivating and believing in me.

DO YOU KNOW WHAT'S A SILENT CLAP?

DO YOU KNOW WHO MOSTLY USES A SILENT CLAP?

DO YOU KNOW HOW TO DO A SILENT CLAP?

DO YOU KNOW ONE OF THE REASONS A SILENT CLAP WAS CREATED?

A SILENT CLAP IS A MOVEMENT OF YOUR HANDS IN A WAVING OR SLIGHT TWIST OF THE WRIST MOTION.

IT CAN BE DONE BY THE SIDES OF YOUR BODY, AROUND THE SHOULDERS OR FACE HEIGHT AND SOMETIMES SLIGHTLY ABOVE YOUR HEAD.

It is an action to show applause.

However, a person who is not deaf, hard of hearing, deaf/blind, or nonverbal can also use a 'silent clap'.

* nonverbal

This is why some people use a 'silent clap'.

* during or after a celebration for a speech or play

One of the reasons 'silent clap' was created is for the deaf, hard of hearing, or deaf/blind to be aware when an applause is happening. The deaf and hard of hearing person could sometimes not hear an applause but will see the gesture or movement of a 'silent clap'.

For those who are deaf/blind, they can feel the movement or gesture of someone who is doing a " silent clap". The slight movement or twisting of the wrists is an indication.

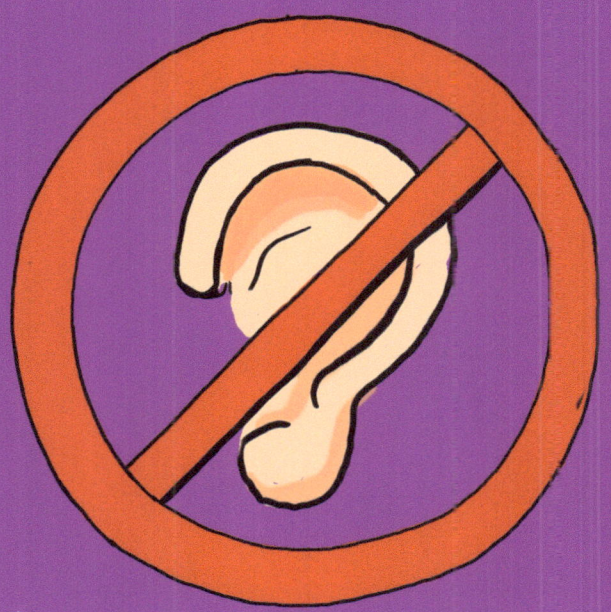

* Unable to hear clapping   * unable to see clapping

When doing a 'silent clap', you usually twist your wrists 3-4 times or continue twisting your wrists until you decide to stop doing the applause.

Twist your wrists 3 times.

You can do a 'silent clap' anywhere! You can silent clap at church, at school, or at a football game.

Do you know how to do a silent clap? Here are some ways.

1. Hold your hands in the air above your head and twist your wrists a few times.

2. Hold your hands up at your ear level and twist your wrists a few times.

3. Position your hands to the side of your body and twist your wrists a few times.

Where would you like to do a silent clap?

* at a game

* at school

* at church

* after a reading

* at the movies

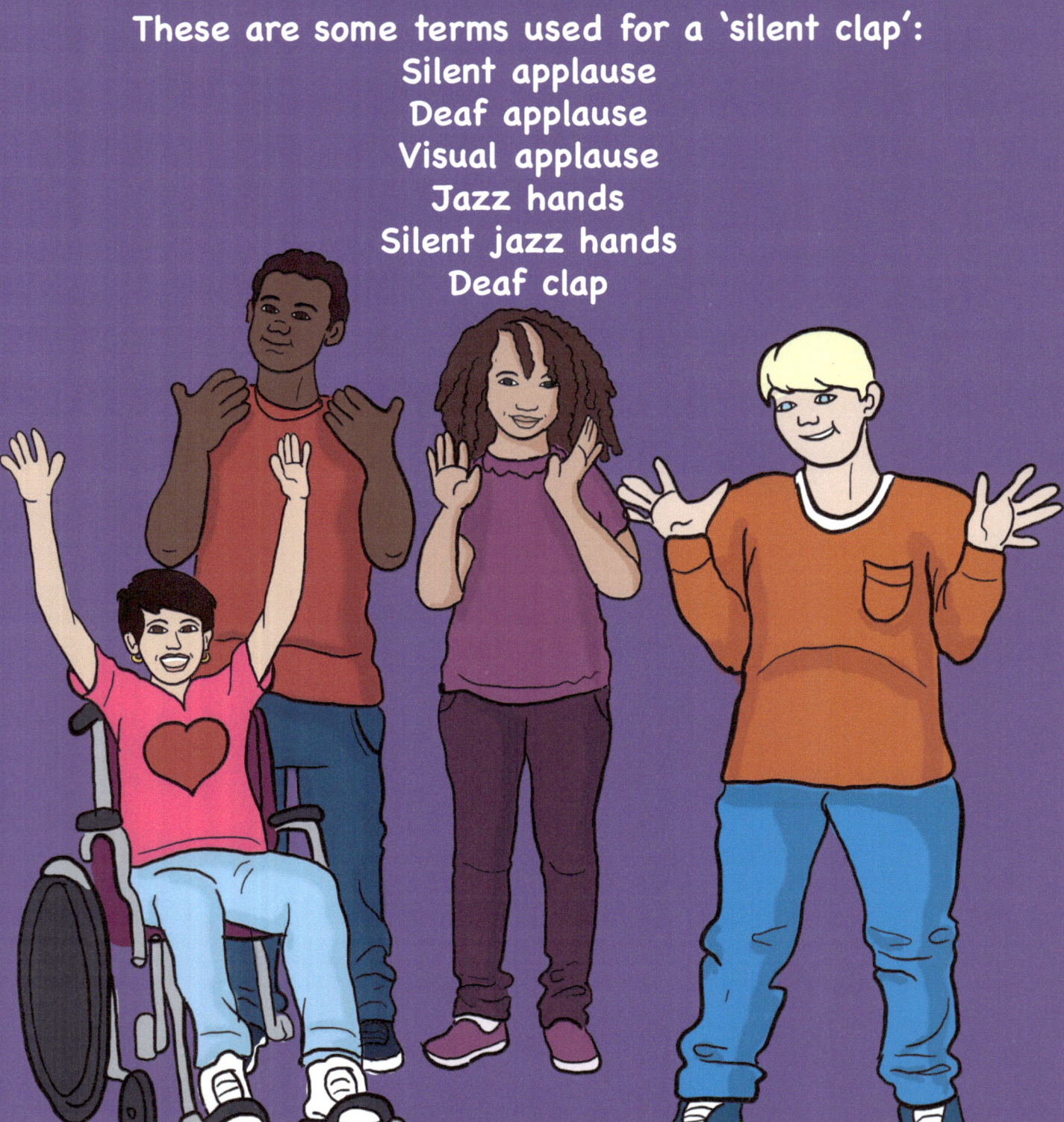

These are some different sign languages used around the world by different countries.

BSL — BLACK SIGN LANGUAGE

JSL — JAMAICAN SIGN LANGUAGE

ASL — AMERICAN SIGN LANGUAGE

ZASL — ZAMBIAN SIGN LANGUAGE

USL — UGANDA SIGN LANGUAGE

KSDSL — KOREAN STANDARD SIGN LANGUAGE

BSL — BRITISH SIGN LANGUAGE

RSL — RUSSIAN SIGN LANGUAGE

PSP — PHILIPPINE SIGN LANGUAGE

NZSL — NEW ZEALAND SIGN LANGUAGE

YSL — YORUBA SIGN LANGUAGE

SASL — SOUTH AFRICA SIGN LANGUAGE

GSE — GHANAIAN SIGN LANGUAGE

Auxiliary sign languages

baby sign – signs used to assist early language development in young children.

Contact Sign – a pidgin or contact language between a spoken language and a sign language, e.g. Pidgin Sign English (PSE).

Curwen Hand Signs – a technique which allows musical notes to be communicated through hand signs.

International Sign (previously known as Gestuno) – an auxiliary language used by deaf people in international settings.

Makaton – a system of signed communication used by and with people who have speech, language or learning difficulties.

Signalong – international sign assisted communication techniques used to support children and adults with communication or learning difficulties.

Additional notes

Sign language was created by the deaf community. It is a natural language for the deaf. Each country has their own version of sign language in which they use to communicate with each other. Some sign languages, however, are signed the same way or similar with the same meaning. Some on the other hand are signed the same but have different meanings.

Vocabulary Terms

HOH   -   Hard Of Hearing

CI   -   Cochlear Implants

www.ingramcontent.com/pod-product-compliance
Lightning Source LLC
Chambersburg PA
CBHW041100070526
44579CB00002B/26